Full of the Deep Bits

Steph Pike

The Knives Forks and Spoons Press
Newton-le-Willows

Published in the United Kingdom in 2010
by The Knives Forks And Spoons Press,
10 Avocet Close,
Newton-le-Willows,
Merseyside,
WA12 9RE.

ISBN 978-0-9563928-7-9

Copyright © Steph Pike, 2010.

The right of Steph Pike to be identified as the author of this work has been asserted by him in accordance with the Copyrights, Designs and Patents act of 1988. All rights reserved. No part of this publication may be reproduced, stored in a retrieval system, transmitted in any form or by any means, electronic, photocopying, recording or otherwise, without prior permission of the publisher.

The cover design is by Alec Newman

Acknowledgements: 'Arran', 'Angel of Anarchy', 'Night out on Arran' and 'Sonnet' were all published in Unsung magazine.

CONTENTS:

Table for Two on Valentine's Night	5
Civil Partnerships and all that Jazz	6
Arran	7
Angel of Anarchy	8
It's Not Black and White	9
God Trains His Angels of Retribution	13
Sea Shore	14
Day Trippers	15
Night Out on Arran	16
Prohibition	17
Piccadilly Gardens	18
Amstetten	19
Sonnet	22
I Want to Fuck David Cameron	23
Age 7	24
Mardi Gras	26
Pantoum	27
Re-claim the Night	28
War on Terror	29
Spanish River	30
Clubbing	32

Table For Two on Valentine's Night

maybe we both hoped that
dressing up and making the effort
would thaw the ice
but instead our hurt
glinted like sharpened knives
in the flickering candlelight
and we glared
at our congealing soup
and ground our food
between clenched teeth

and when i tried to ease the tension
by mentioning my intention
to stab the loved up couple next to us
with my fork
you just stared at me with a look
that was so fed up of me
that i tapped and hummed
swung on my chair
clinked my rings together
did all those small, stupid, nervous things
that once i'd tried so hard to avoid
because they annoyed you

so we scraped back our chairs
and left in separate directions
each without a backward glance
and i knew then, that that night
by severing the fraying thread
that held us together
Cupid and his arrow
had turned assassin
and killed our love stone dead

Civil Partnerships and All that Jazz

we're getting civvied up
we're de-mob happy
the war is through
we're rushing out
to say "i do, i do"
we're very nearly
just like you
we're in the suburbs
with our 4x4s and 2.2
kids. we go on family trips
to International Ladies Day

Hey, times have changed
we've won the right
to become racist thugs in blue
to butch it up in prisons
swing our keys
clank our chains
join the army
we're in the main
stream now
we're getting carried away
we're celebrating this freedom we've found
with our beautiful, shiny, pink pound
we're pushing out the boat
we're afloat at last

are we fuck! we're all at sea
because this isn't a war that we won
we just crossed over to the enemy

Arran

because both birds and whales sing
i lie down and let you run through me
because both birds and whales
i lie down and let you run
through me you sing with
anarchy in your face
my eyes flicker like
side show freaks
and eclipse the setting sun
your anarchy enfolds me
a storm blue sky
where i migrate
to shaking winds
to pods of whales
to fleeting birds
to me

Angel of Anarchy
(Francesca Woodman Photograph – Untitled, Rome, Italy 1977 – 1978)

i've taken this space
the apron's gone
the clean floor mine for once
i'm jesus am i
or a suicide
it's not for you to decide
i'm not nailed up here by your desire
no sacrificial lamb
strong, i hang by my fingers
head to one side
you think i'm dead, or depressed
you're wrong
i'm a bird on a branch
an acrobat, a free diver
an angel about to take flight

i've thrown my face
the apron's skirt masks me
the floor rancid all the time
am i not satan
or a birth
it's for you to divine
i'm strung up by your apathy
a blood sacrifice
weakened, my nails tear
my head too heavy for my neck
you think that i'm happy, enjoy this
i'm a bird in a cage
petrified, a sinking stone
an angel without wings

It's Not Black and White

in my head it's every day
it happens every day
in my head
it won't go away
i can't make it
a film playing
over and over
as if i didn't care
as if i could forget
what i did
on those days
all those years ago
what else can i do
but think
shut in here
what else can i do
but have the inside of my head
become a film theatre
become a cassette player
those tapes on a constant loop
that i helped make
my chickens come home to roost
there's no shooing them away
the film playing constantly
on the back of my eyes
sleep is no relief
i dream of it
the slow drip of blood
in my head
my own doing
my own fault
as though i could forget
it's not black and white
a full colour horror
flick of my soul
of what i did
all those years ago

i look in the mirror
all i see is that picture
black and white
through the red haze
filming my eyes
it's not the spots of blood
that won't wash off
it's the bloody film
on your eyes
that no amount of tears
can wash clear
i can only see myself
through their eyes now
that one image
i know i've aged
my face has changed
got softer i'd say
i've kept my hair it's
natural colour
but i stare and i stare
at the mirror
and all i see is
peroxide blond
black eyes
cheekbones
hard granite slabs
that overlook the place
they died
it was me

in my head it's every day
have i changed
is my heart still
a shock of barbed wire
did all the education
all the religion
give me wisdom
or just a mask

to trick them
and me
they've got to me
evil breathing in
a prison gown
or human
who has grown
remorseful
shown that hope
is possible

to them i'll always be
black and white
woman in negative
born bad
too evil to
go mad
they keep me young
the screams
ringing in their ears
for years
the papers kept it up
til i died
my body dead
but that image
goes on and on
they made a ghost of me
when my life
had barely begun

not that i'm complaining
i don't have the right
but i did change
and the redemption
wouldn't just
be for me
humanity would benefit
in some strange way
we're all de-humanised
along the way

i was a mirror
they wanted to smash
into splinters so small
they couldn't see
the possibility
the reality
of their own
inhumanity
it wasn't the differences
it was the similarities
that made them
throw away the key
that made them
want to kill me

God Trains His Angels of Retribution

they rolled up on a train
at a place which was like a holiday camp
but the showers were strange
and the food was bad
and they had to provide the entertainment
and the lighting

afterwards, everyone agreed
that it must have been hell
god was satisfied
and smiled bewitchingly

Sea Shore

she sought pebbles on the sea's shore
she padded her print on the sea's shore
she pebbled the sea with her tears
she sought her pebbled tears
and the print of her soul
on the seeing sea's shore
she saw her soul on the shore of the sea
she saw a shoal of her tears
flash in the shoulder of the sea
her wept tears swept onto the sea's shore
and glistened in the sand
she knelt, and felt her sadness solid in her hand
she felt her sadness solid in her hand
she knelt, and the sand shored her
she knelt, and the sea swept her
her soul found her on the sea's shore
her tears flowed free
her fear ebbed, with the ebbing of the sea

Day Trippers

gulls shriek
we burst onto the seafront
hearts juddering like bus engines
laughing, we shovel crisps into
mouths too ravenous to shut
against the blowing sand

blue melts into yellow
the end of the summer
washes our backs with warmth
and your fingers rippling my hair

later, you dribble alien
words and someone else's
half-eaten spring roll into my ear
and I know we're
on the slow train home
half-cut and happy

Night Out on Arran

Disco Dave has shingles tonight
sweats rusty water
projects psychedelic flowers
on Eden's walls
her hair suits this light
so she stays out
deep into the night
drinking a toast to
her head's hot halo
then shimmers home
while the still sea
whispers otters' secrets
and mussels snigger
like knuckle cracks

Prohibition

Leah Betts drowned
she had green hair
and star fish in her eyes

twenty years before his time
she paints with Marc Almond on her palette
and sex dwarves on her mind

you wear her shrunken head
around your neck
and still that thing you call a sofa

chews your leg
while Crimewatch
tells you not to dream at night

Ecstasy never beat me to death
in my own home.
go on then; one more drink for the road

Piccadilly Gardens

children play in fluting streams
watched by men whose pants
are cast from cold wrought iron
to hide the tell-tale signs
that unleashed, punch 999
into frantic fathers' minds
who report 'robbery'
their exclusive property
coveted by other men's preying eyes

the green and purple kaleidoscopic clouds
of starlings' swirling evening cabaret
are years gone
replaced by metal birds
that roost with hard unblinking eye
static observers of urban life
the city turned voyeurs' paradise

in the cooling rain
night slides down
shadows shift and slink away
the children move like moths
drawn by bleeping squat
machines dispensing dreams
 of fame and unknown wealth
the 10p thrill of a neon pleasure dome
safer here than in their homes

Amstetten

it was all Julie Andrews
and alpine meadows
big cream cakes and rosy-faced people
and blue skies with fluffy clouds
and soft brown cows with clanking bells
and clean air and Edelweiss
all pretty and cosy and nice
until one fine, upstanding Austrian man
took his daughter by the hand
and shut her up

Amstetten, hang your head in shame
Austria, hang your head in shame

we've taken the lid off
your chocolate box land
and found your dirty soul

suddenly, the green of the alpine grass
the blue of the cloudless sky
the child's beaming yellow sun
are too perfect, too bright
their coffee and cake sticks in our throat
the cows are a greek chorus
with bells of doom
we hate their too clean streets
their lawns without a blade of grass mis-placed
a neurotic people in the home of freud
everything too tidy, too fake
a plastic people
programmed for evil
their outrages subterranean
hidden below their toy-town houses
and smiling, yodelling faces

even the Austrians join in this national flagellation
their police and psychiatrists parading on TV
basking in their 5 minutes of fame
pondering, who's to blame for this atrocity?
is there something in the post-war
nazi-loving Austrian psyche?

because we're shocked, we're at a loss
we can't understand how this has happened

and i think, Bullshit!
this talk of Austrian blame
is a magician's trick, a sleight of hand
an illusionist's game of mis-direction

because i look around me
and i see

women naked in cages
in adult clubs
and women naked on pages
in papers and mags
and nose jobs
and boob jobs
and a nip
and a vaginal tuck
to give men a
perfect fitting fuck
and daddy giving
his little princess
a long kiss goodnight
and thousands of women abused
in our modern civilised society
where 95% of rapists go free

and we don't understand how Amstetten happened

girls in pink
and boys in blue
genders assigned
so we don't get confused
so that boys can be boys
and girls know their place
slag, whore
slapper, cunt
wolf whistles
and show us your tits
and suck my cock
you fucking bitch

and we don't understand how Amstetten happened

Sonnet

heaven slams its rusty gates
the xanthine glow of the neon sign
barks 'Shut' into the salty faces of the dead
the perished mob is brass bold
defenestrates their treacherous god and
flows behind, a ghostly mist
to seal his fate in grey cement.
the family on the patio are oblivious
share pizza and beers
cocooned in the paraphernalia of a summer afternoon
their limbs entwined in knots
the bricks of their home cling close
to demonstrate the nuclear way is fine
whilst the reactor nearby coughs death into the air

I Want to Fuck David Cameron

i want to fuck David Cameron
i want to be the divine Mrs. C
i want to tweak his ruddy cheeks
run my fingers through his thinning beige hair
rub my body all over his
sliced white-dough physique
i want to wear a twin-set in pastel blue
ride with him on his
environmentally-friendly bicycle for two
i'm going to wear a hoody, just so
he'll hug me and fill me with his Tory love
i want to be a single mother
i want to be poor, i want to be needy
anything, so he'll use me
in a moving photo opportunity
oh yes Davey my new Tory mate
i really thought you'd turned me straight, except
i want to fuck Margaret Thatcher too
i saw her down Lash for Lasses
suited and booted wit her concrete hair and that
"come to bed, or i'll break your fucking neck" stare
oh, those Tories have got me so wet
they've gone all lovey-dovey, touchy-feely
they are such sexy Dulux dogs
they've gone all blue with a hint of green
blue with a hint of pink
blue with a hint of black
blue with a hint of any fucking tint
that'll lure those voters little kisses in
you see, they've got me so confused
i used to know where i stood
the evil Tories were bad
and Labour, well they were kind of, sort of good
but now they've all merged
into one head-fuck toxic mix
of rightwing, capitalist war-mongering shits
and i'm so loved up that all i want to do is give
each and every one of them a great big Kirby kiss

Age 7

it was the year of that dress
a lemon-meringue mess
of yellow nylon
and white lace trim

in that dress
she was not the girl
who bent a paper-clip
and felt the whip of your hand
on her face

in that dress
she was not the girl
who threw her first punch
and heard the satisfying crunch
of her sister's nose

in that dress
she was not the girl
you chased with a belt
and who, for the first time
smelt her own fear

in that dress
she was not the girl
who disappointed your days
with her strange
and awkward ways

in that dress
she was all things nice
sugar and spice
her mother's pride
the apple of her daddy's eye

in that dress
she was straight-jacket calm
good as gold
with folded arms and knees closed
who tried and tried to please

she was your bees knees

that was the year
a little girl
in a bile-yellow dress
waiting to explode

Mardi Gras

when i see the 'Fish n Chips and PG Tips'
stall roll into town
i know it's time to dust down
my lesbian uniform
to get a funky crop
on the top of my head
perfect for copping off with women
whose faces i won't recognise
and names i won't remember
by the end of Monday night
i'll put on my favourite combats
with all its pockets and zips
where i'll hide the stash of
coke and Es and whizz
that i'll need to ignore
the army of straights
who've invaded our space;
that i'll need to cheer the parade
and laugh and clap
as they throw their corporate tat
and to believe that i do really look great
in my 'Barclays Loves Gay Bankers' baseball cap
and i'll need more drugs just to
cope once again with Hazel Dean
and the endless stream
of Z-list celebs scrambling on stage
for their sweet piece of the Mardi Gras cake
because someone's found the pot of gold
at the end of our rainbow nation's
weekend extravaganza of capitalist exploitation
and i wonder – is this what it was for
is this why we protested, marched on the streets
got spat on and arrested
is this what happened to gay liberation
our dreams lying in a canal street gutter
buried in rubbish and cold chips
bleeding hope and stinking of puke and stale piss

Pantoum

the fish had drowned at dawn
rejected by the earth it longed to die
caught by the sun's first yawn
silver scales reflected in the sky

rejected by the earth it longed to die
lilies hung their heavy heads in grief
silver scales reflected in the sky
whispered scandal carried on the breeze

lilies hung their heavy heads in grief
this water creature could not accept its fate
whispered scandal carried on the breeze
the morning rain had mocked its liquid state

this water creature could not accept its fate
caught by the sun's first yawn
the morning rain had mocked its liquid state
the fish had drowned at dawn

Re-claim the Night

along avenues and boulevards
tree-lined streets and winding roads
down country lanes and muddy tracks
in shadowed alleys and cul-de-sacs
on narrow trails through
lonely woods and urban parks
on long routes, short routes
disused rail routes
across wasteland, parkland
farmland; our land
whether city bright or
dark as the night itself
these streets are ours

walking sober and sedate
or stumbling home late
binge-drunk on alcopops and
off our heads on Class A drugs
in sturdy boots or 6 inch heels
in skirts so short and tops slung low
or wrapped up warm against the cold
glammed up, dressed down
made up, veiled up
on the piss or on the pull
in raucous groups and all alone
these streets are ours

homeless, turning tricks
to meet a mate, or just for kicks
to sit beneath the stars and moon
and know that soon
the sun will rise upon us still alive
because sleep evades us
because a whim takes us
because we choose to go
wherever we like
at any time of day or night
to know the twilight, midnight, dawnlight hours
these streets are ours

War on Terror

walking home each night, the same picture
the dead soldier has been informed
deliberate and surgical, a blow to the heart
the electronic wailing of a woman
must shut them down
precision missiles and a spate of
roadside bombs play in the street
the shrug of a cold shoulder

dead

like a winter morning
like a shallow afternoon
like an evening drowned
the government paying tribute
crouches like a cancer
staring through unbreakable glass
grimy with fear, i sing the low moan
of apache helicopters clattering for blood

Spanish River

she stands, cigarette smokes
Spanish river flows
still, past her calves i'd seen
earlier, at the top of her stare
i said something – ravine –
had heard her
feel where the stare turns
becoming one of blatant river in the sun
catch her eyes, softening
clear green water
and her two easy boys
relaxed moons
around her orbit
warming me

me at her centre
sun on my back she takes me
her slippery skin
under my hands hauling me
a waterfall high through the water
up in the river, 'swim' she says
we glide over a clear middle
of the narrow, crystal pool
deep as her, rushing river, swimming heart
and my toes full of the deep bits
of nothing but shivers
and she gives me this
water high as our thighs
through, always through the clambering
wading, scrambling rocks
the ache in my muscles
feels bursting with pride of her
following the bigness,
arms up, fingers gripping of her back
her shoulders moss-rock rolling
her planting feet thundering the water
over our soaking bodies

the edge
and with our shoulders, the choice
she by my side
parting the water
falls like a raindrop in great sheets
like a tear
like life dancing in my eyes
the edge and the turn
and the throw of myself
deep in, through her space
the green clear is all surface
of the around me silent pool
and she is there
and down becomes us
and with a watching smile
me on a rock
and she on the shore

Clubbing

poledancing is great exercise, right?
and lapdancing is just girls having sexy fun
lapdancing clubs outnumber rape crisis centres three to one

no. nothing about any of this is right
erotic dancing is women's power
car-crashed, pole-wrapped
bodies distorted and cash-strapped
souls slapped, men's eyes glued
like traps, demanding 'gyrate!'
while women's lives are drowned out
in the dingy, thumping bass beat of hate

and my heart would crack
except I know that feminism is lazarus
and rises back stronger
each time they pronounce it dead

and I long, I long
to break the seals of the sea
so that gentlemen's clubs are drowned in silt
so that starfish flood the land
and dance in wonder by our feet
so that women float majestic like icebergs
down urban highways and suburban streets

www.ingramcontent.com/pod-product-compliance
Ingram Content Group UK Ltd.
Pitfield, Milton Keynes, MK11 3LW, UK
UKHW041958101025
463832UK00011B/34